World in Focus
Ireland

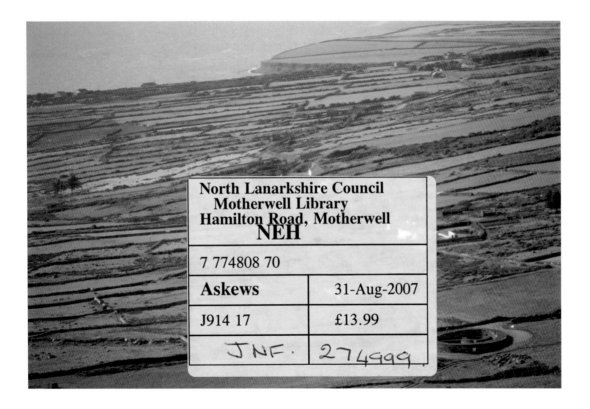

ROB BOWDEN AND RONAN FOLEY

WAYLAND

First published in 2007 by Wayland, an imprint of Hachette Children's Books

Hachette Children's Books, 338 Euston Road, London NW1 3BH

Wayland Australia, Hachette Children's Books, Level 17/207 Kent Street, Sydney, NSW 2000

Commissioning editor: Nicola Edwards
Editor: Nicola Barber
Inside design: Chris Halls, www.mindseyedesign.co.uk
Cover design: Hodder Wayland
Series concept and project management by EASI-Educational Resourcing
(info@easi-er.co.uk)

Statistical research: Anna Bowden
Maps and graphs: Martin Darlison, Encompass Graphics
Printed and bound in China

Bowden, Rob
  Ireland. - (World in focus)
  1.Ireland - Juvenile literature
  I.Title II.Foley, Ronan
  941.7'0824

ISBN-13: 9780750247450

Cover top: Hurling is a popular Gaelic sport in Ireland.
Cover bottom: King John's Castle in Limerick stands on the banks of the River Shannon.
Title page: Irish landscape in County Kerry.

The author and publisher would like to thank the following for allowing their pictures to be reproduced in this publication:
Corbis 6, 24, 34, 36, 46, 47 (Reuters), 8 (Gianni Dagli Orti), 10 (Corbis), 11, 41 (PictureNet Corporation), 12, 23 (Paul McErlane/epa), 13, 31, 42 (Gideon Mendel), 14, 22, 55, 56 (Michael St Maur Sheil), 19, 32, 39 (Richard Cummins), 35 (Alessandra Benedetti), 37 (Justin Kernoghan/epa), 38 (Geray Sweeney), 43 (Michael Short/Robert Harding World Imagery), 52 (Felix Zaska), 58 (Jason Hawkes), 59 (Howard Davies); EASI-Images cover, title page, 4, 5, 15, 16, 17, 18, 20, 21, 25, 26, 28, 29, 30, 33, 40, 44, 48, 49, 50, 51, 54, 57 (Chris Fairclough/CFW Images), 27, 53 (Rob Bowden); Getty Images 45 (Chris Maddaloni/AFP); Mary Evans Picture Library 9.

The website addresses (URLs) included in this book were valid at the time of going to press. However, because of the nature of the Internet, it is possible that some addresses may have changed, or sites may have changed or closed down since publication. While the author and Publishers regret any inconvenience this may cause the readers, no responsibility for any such changes can be accepted by either the author or the Publisher.

The directional arrow portrayed on the map on page 7 provides only an approximation of north.

The data used to produce the graphics and data panels in this title were the latest available at the time of production.

CONTENTS

CHAPTER 1

Ireland – An Overview

The island of Ireland is situated to the west of Great Britain and is the most westerly landmass in Europe after Iceland. An ancient land steeped in folklore and legends, Ireland was under British control until the island was split into two in 1921. The northern counties remained part of the United Kingdom (UK) and are today known as Northern Ireland. The southern counties (accounting for around 85 per cent of the landmass) formed a new nation, the Irish Free State, renamed Eire in 1937 and then the Republic of Ireland in 1949.

TURBULENT INFANCY

Many people were unhappy with the terms of the treaty that established the Irish Free State and kept Northern Ireland as a separate state within the United Kingdom. Civil war broke out in 1921, ending in 1923 with victory for the Irish Free State (see page 12). There continue to be widely different views on the split between Ireland and Northern Ireland.

The political separation of Ireland from Northern Ireland was only one element of Ireland's turbulent infancy as an independent state. Years of depopulation (see page 19) saw many of Ireland's most educated citizens

▼ The Dingle peninsula between Clogher Head and Sybil Head in County Kerry. Ireland's Atlantic coastline is both dramatic and rugged.

emigrate, particularly to the UK and the United States, leaving the country depleted of labour. In fact, there are today thought to be at least as many Irish people living abroad as there are in Ireland. The first decades of independence also witnessed dramatic economic changes as traditional industries went into decline. Rising unemployment and urban decay became a feature of many of Ireland's cities.

A COUNTRY TRANSFORMED

In 1965, Ireland signed trade agreements with the UK and then, in 1973, became a member of the European Union (EU) (called the European Economic Community (EEC) until 1992). These acts began the transformation of Ireland into a modern economy and one of the wealthiest nations in Europe. Membership of the EU brought Ireland millions of dollars worth of grants to improve its infrastructure and create new employment opportunities. Since then, traditional industries such as mining, textiles and food processing have been replaced with high-tech electronics, pharmaceuticals, software development and a thriving service industry. EU membership provided new trading opportunities for Irish goods and made the country an attractive base for overseas companies, particularly from the United States, with which Ireland has close connections through its history of emigration.

The changing fortunes of Ireland have seen its population increase from around 3 million in 1973 to 4.1 million in 2005. This represents an increase of 32.4 per cent, compared with just 6.5 per cent in the UK over the same period. Much of this population growth is due to Irish people returning from overseas, but recent years have seen considerable new waves of immigration from Asia and Europe in particular. The expansion of the EU from 15 (until 2004) to 27 members by 2007 has further influenced this trend, and Ireland expects to receive many immigrants from the new member countries over the coming years.

▲ A new retail and office complex takes shape in the centre of Limerick. Ireland's booming construction industry is one of the most obvious symbols of its recent growth and success.

NEW CHALLENGES

Having survived political upheavals and the restructuring of its economy, Ireland today faces new challenges. Some of these are as a result of its recent success and include a rapid rise in the cost of living (particularly house prices) and severe traffic congestion as more people buy their own vehicles. Irish culture is also under pressure with global forces diluting some traditions and making the Irish language a rarity outside the rural west. Thankfully, an increase in tourism is helping to create new interest in Irish culture, enabling artforms such as music and dance to undergo a resurgence in popularity both within and beyond Ireland. The Irish are a proud people with a strong sense of identity, but as their country continues to diversify and change, this identity will undergo fresh challenges to define the Ireland of the 21st century.

Physical geography

- Land area: 68,890 sq km / 26,598 sq miles
- Water area: 1,390 sq km / 537 sq miles
- Total area: 70,280 sq km / 27,135 sq miles
- World rank (by area): 121
- Land boundaries: 360 km / 224 miles
- Border countries: United Kingdom
- Coastline: 1,448 km / 900 miles
- Highest point: Carrauntoohil (1,041 m / 3,415 ft)
- Lowest point: Atlantic Ocean (0 m / 0 ft)

Source: CIA World Factbook

A dancer with the Inishowen Carnival Group dances during the St Patrick's Day Parade in Dublin. St Patrick's Day (17 March) is celebrated every year.

ATLANTIC OCEAN

NORTHERN IRELAND (to UK)

Letterkenny

DONEGAL

Killybegs Donegal

Donegal Bay

Erris Head

Sligo

SLIGO

Lough Conn *Lough Allen*

MONAGHAN

Achill Island

LEITRIM

Dundalk

CAVAN

Dundalk Bay

LOUTH

Irish Sea

Castlebar

MAYO ROSCOMMON LONGFORD

Boyne Drogheda

Navan

Lough Mask

C o n n a u g h t

Lough Ree

Mullingar MEATH

Swords

TWELVE BENS

Lough Corrib

WESTMEATH

Leixlip

DUBLIN

Connemara

Athlone

GALWAY

REPUBLIC OF

Celbridge Dún Laoghaire

DUBLIN

Galway

OFFALY

Naas Bray

Galway Bay

Newbridge

KILDARE

Aran Islands

Shannon

IRELAND

WICKLOW MOUNTAINS

LAOIS *Wicklow Head*

L e i n s t e r

WICKLOW

CLARE *Lough Derg*

Ennis

Carlow Arklow

CARLOW

ATLANTIC OCEAN

Limerick

Kilkenny

Loop Head

Mouth of the Shannon

LIMERICK

TIPPERARY KILKENNY

WEXFORD

Tralee

M u n s t e r

Clonmel *Suir*

Wexford

Rosslare

KERRY

Waterford

St George's Channel

Blackwater WATERFORD

Dingle Bay Killarney CORK

Carrauntoohil 1,041 m ▲

MACGILLYCUDDY'S REEKS

Cork

Celtic Sea

N

0   40   80 kilometres
0   20   40 miles

Legend

★ Capital
● Cities > 100,000
● Cities > 50,000
● Cities > 25,000
· other cities
▲ Mountain

CHAPTER 2

History

Ireland's ancient history is rich and colourful, interwoven with elements of folklore and legend as much as known fact.

PRE-HISTORY AND THE VIKINGS

Archaeological finds provide evidence of a number of ancient tribes who lived in Ireland as far back as 6000-5000 BC. One of the greatest pre-history sites is the great burial monument of Newgrange in the Boyne Valley (*Brú na Boinne*), built in around 3200 BC. The Hill of Tara is another well known archaeological monument and was traditionally the seat of Ireland's early kings.

Ireland was known to the Romans as Hibernia, but the Romans never formally attempted a conquest of the country. Instead, Ireland became a Celtic country, sharing strong cultural and linguistic traits with other Celtic regions such as Wales, northern England and Scotland. For example, Ireland's patron saint, St Patrick, came from Wales and is credited with bringing Christianity to Ireland in around AD 432.

From the 9th to the 11th centuries Ireland was invaded by Vikings, from Scandinavia. The Vikings were known for their ferocity and regularly raided the Irish countryside. They founded a coastal settlement in Ireland which they called *Dubh Linn*, meaning 'Black Pool'. In time this was to become Ireland's largest city and capital, Dublin. It was near Dublin, at the Battle at Clontarf in 1014, that the combined Irish forces led by the last High King of Ireland, Brian Boru, managed finally to defeat the Vikings.

ENGLISH RULE

Following the defeat of the Vikings in 1014, Ireland remained divided amongst a number of warring chieftains. One of these chieftains,

◄ The view down the internal passageway of the Newgrange burial monument in the Boyne Valley.

Diarmuid McMurrough, requested help from King Henry II of England, resulting in the arrival of Anglo-Norman soldiers in 1169 and the start of an English presence in Ireland. The role and dominance of the English in Ireland increased slowly and steadily until by the 13th century England ruled much of the country. The English had direct control over Dublin and the surrounding area, but governed the rest of Ireland through a series of uneasy truces with various tribal chieftains.

The unease of these relationships led to rebellions against English rule, the first of which occurred in Donegal and Tyrone in the early 16th century. The rebellion was put down, but led the English to take a more direct approach to rule, giving large land grants to English and Scottish interests in order to extend their reach and influence. The Great Plantation of Ulster (1610s), where Scottish settlers were particularly prominent, was the largest of these land allocations and led to the creation of a large Protestant and Presbyterian colony in the north of Ireland. Other plantations were established in the west and south of the country (1550s), and especially in the Queen's and King's counties (now Laois and Offaly).

For the next century, relations between the Irish and their English rulers continued to deteriorate, leading to another major revolt in the mid-17th century. The English sent Oliver Cromwell and his army to restore control. The English army burned a number of towns, including Drogheda, in revenge for the revolt. English rule became more forceful still and included the strong suppression of native language, culture and religion through the Penal Laws. These laws were in place from the the late 17th century until Catholic

▲ A scene depicting the Drogheda massacre in 1649. Oliver Cromwell led the English forces as they besieged the town and killed around 3,000 people in punishment for a rebellion against English control.

emancipation in 1829 (see page 10) and effectively banned Catholicism and the speaking of the Irish language in public. Catholicism remained strong during this period, but the decline in everyday use of the Irish language (*Gaelige* or Gaelic) can be traced back to this time.

IRELAND 1780-1900

Under growing pressure, the British government allowed a notional Irish parliament throughout the 18th century, culminating in the short-lived Grattan's Parliament founded in 1785. Following a further uprising in 1798, the 1801 Act of Union made Ireland a part of the United Kingdom. This formalization of rule allowed direct representation of Irish interests, led by statesmen such as Daniel O'Connell (1775-1847), and saw a reduction in the suppression of the Irish. The Catholic emancipation of 1829, when Catholics were finally given the right to vote, is an example of these greater freedoms.

Relations between Britain and the Irish were soon tested again however, this time by a natural disaster. The 'Great Famine' of 1845-7 saw Ireland's potato crop fail dramatically due to a blight disease (see box on page 19). Britain's reaction was ineffectual and late, leading to a famine in which over a million people died of starvation and another million fled the country. The famine renewed resentment towards the British and led to further uprisings in 1848 and 1867, the latter led by a group called the Fenians whose aim was Irish independence. The Fenian leaders were exiled to Australia but continued to influence Irish politicians within the British parliament to press for Irish home rule. Led by John Redmond and Charles Stuart Parnell the Fenian movement became very active in London during the 1880s. In Ireland a parallel movement called the Land League, led by Michael Davitt, pushed forward a programme of land nationalization and the reduction of the power of the Anglo-Irish gentry.

FROM HOME RULE TO THE FREE STATE

As Ireland entered the new century, Britain's control over the country was weakening due to the pressure for home rule. The exception to this was in the north of Ireland which, through its mostly Protestant population (the majority of

◀ A poor Irish family searches desperately for potatoes during the Great Famine of 1845-7. The famine was caused by the almost complete failure of Ireland's potato crop.

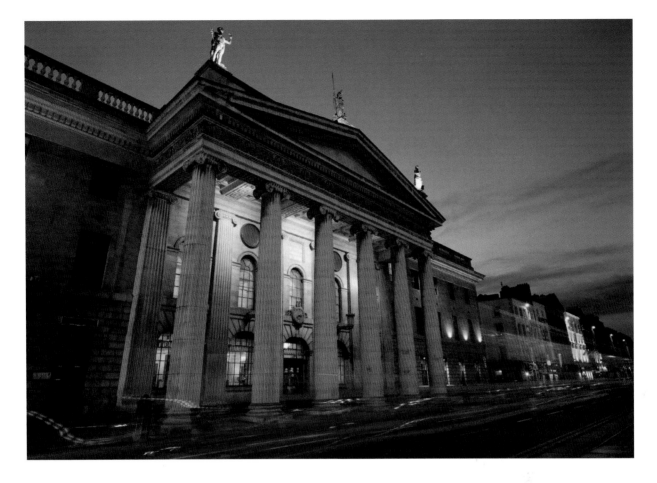

▲ The General Post Office in Dublin was the main base for the rebels during the April 1916 uprising.

Ireland's people were Catholic), was loyal to British rule. The British recognized that home rule for Ireland was inevitable and plans to implement it were mostly agreed in 1912, but then delayed due to the outbreak of World War I (in 1914).

While Britain was distracted by World War I, the Fenians and a new organization, the Irish Republican Brotherhood (IRB), took the opportunity to mount a rebellion. They were committed to creating a fully independent, all-Ireland republic. One of the leaders of the IRB, Pádraig Pearse, led the rebels as they occupied the General Post Office and other prominent Dublin buildings in April 1916. The rebels held out for a week before surrendering to the British. Pearse and most of the other leaders of the failed rebellion were executed by firing squad. Only two were spared: Countess Markiewicz, because she was a woman, and Eamon de Valera (a future *Taoiseach* (prime minister) and president), because he was born in the United States.

After World War I, Irish interests became increasingly unified under the leadership of the political party Sinn Féin (We Ourselves). Sinn Féin used this support to declare the first independent *Dáil* (parliament) of Ireland, an act that led to the War of Independence between Britain and Ireland in 1919-21. A ceasefire was agreed in 1921 and negotiations began which led to the creation of the Irish Free State.

Focus on: The Irish partition

The negotiations for Ireland's independence proved to be a key point in Irish history. The main issue was the refusal of over a million Protestants in Ulster to surrender British rule for a Catholic-dominated Irish state. The response, negotiated by Michael Collins and others, was to sign a treaty of partition with the British in December 1921. This treaty guaranteed a form of independence for the 26 southern counties as the 'Irish Free State'. It excluded the six counties of Northern Ireland which would have a level of independent control within the British state. However, the treaty led almost immediately to the Irish Civil War (1922-3). Michael Collins and Kevin O'Higgins led the Irish Free State against Eamon de Valera and Sinn Féin republicans who wanted a 32-county Irish Republic, completely independent from Britain. Michael Collins was assassinated during the course of the civil war, which was finally won by the Irish Free State.

THE TROUBLES OF THE NORTH

Southern Ireland gained full independence in 1949 and formally became the Republic of Ireland. Meanwhile, Northern Ireland remained part of the United Kingdom, a position supported by the majority Protestant population and broadly opposed by the minority Catholic population. Up until the 1960s life was relatively peaceful in the north, but things changed dramatically during that decade. At this time, political and economic power in Northern Ireland lay mainly in the hands of the Protestant majority. Many of the Catholic minority felt discriminated against and, following the example of African-Americans in the United States, began to call for equal rights.

◀ These burnt-out cars are a result of troubles in August 2006 between Protestants and Catholics in the mainly Catholic region of Bogside in Londonderry, Northern Ireland. Incidents like this are a reminder of the delicate peace that exists in Northern Ireland.

▲ An assembly line for Dell computers in Limerick. Many high-tech industries have chosen to establish manufacturing and assembly operations in Ireland.

The first Civil Rights marches of 1968-9 led to resistance from members of the Protestant community, who were concerned that the movement might result in their becoming a part of a united, Catholic-dominated Ireland. Tensions between the Protestant and Catholic communities escalated with increasing violence between the two communities until, in 1969, the British Army was brought in to restore peace.

There was no peace, however. Instead the two sides developed paramilitary movements determined to fight their cause through whatever means, including violence. The Irish Republican Army (IRA) became the main Catholic paramilitary group, whilst the Ulster Volunteer Force (UVF) and Ulster Defence Force (UDF) were among those fighting the Protestant cause. The violence between the two communities, known as 'The Troubles', was at its worst during the 1970s when daily bombings and killings spread beyond Northern Ireland into the Republic of Ireland and mainland UK. Violence continued into the 1980s and beyond, only slowing following political discussions and the 1993 'Downing Street Declaration' that guaranteed Protestants a vote in any potential unification. In 1994 the IRA announced a ceasefire, but the true cessation of violence and the decommissioning of weapons did not take place until autumn 2005, following more than a decade of negotiation.

RECOVERY IN THE SOUTH

Despite the violence in Northern Ireland, the Republic of Ireland has remained politically stable. It suffered major economic problems during the 1970s and 1980s, but emerged in the 1990s as one of the fastest-growing and wealthiest economies in Europe. The economic boom has slowed a little since 2000, but Ireland continues to outpace many European rivals and is today a modern, wealthy and increasingly cosmopolitan country.

CHAPTER 3

Landscape and Climate

Ireland covers a total area of 70,280 sq km (27,135 sq miles) which makes it smaller than all but ten US states, and slightly smaller than Scotland in the UK. It shares a 360-km (224-mile) border with Northern Ireland (part of the UK) to the north, but is otherwise surrounded by the Atlantic Ocean – called the Irish Sea in the stretch of water between Ireland and Great Britain.

COASTAL HIGHLANDS

Physically Ireland can be thought of as a saucer shape with coastal highlands forming the perimeter and a mainly flat depression towards the centre. The highest point in these coastal highlands is Carrauntoohil at 1,041 m (3,415 ft) in the Macgillycuddy's Reeks range of County Kerry, southwest Ireland. The Macgillycuddy's Reeks contain a further eight of the ten highest peaks in Ireland. Other significant highlands include the Wicklow Mountains south of Dublin and the Twelve Bens range in County Galway, western Ireland.

In the southwest of Ireland the highlands jut into the Atlantic Ocean forming a series of jagged peninsulas separated by rias (former river valleys now drowned beneath the ocean). A good example of a ria is the bay of Dingle in

▼ Tourists admire the dramatic Slieve League cliffs on the Atlantic Ocean near Carrick, County Donegal.

County Kerry. In County Donegal, northwestern Ireland, the highlands plunge into the sea in dramatic fashion at the sea cliffs of Slieve League. At 595 m (1,952 ft) , Slieve League is one of the highest sea cliffs in Europe. The west coast is also characterized by a number of offshore islands, most of them small and uninhabited. Some larger ones, such as Achill at 146 sq km (57 sq miles), are occupied. In sharp contrast to the west, Ireland's east coast is less rugged and has a number of gentle bays. Several of Ireland's most important ports are located along this eastern coastline including Dublin, Drogheda and Rosslare.

WATERWAYS

Ireland's longest river, the River Shannon, rises at Shannon Pot in County Cavan and flows

▲ The River Shannon as it flows into Limerick, with the 13th-century King John's Castle in the background. West of Limerick, the Shannon flows into its estuary which extends 113 km (70 miles) to the Atlantic Ocean.

south for around 260 km (162 miles) to the Atlantic Ocean west of Limerick. Though not of great length, the River Shannon drains almost a quarter of Ireland's land area. With so much water passing through it, the river spills into marshes and bogs along much of its length and forms small lakes in several places. In total Ireland has over 11,000 lakes, most of them formed by glaciers during the last Ice Age. The lakes are well known for their salmon and trout populations.

MILD CLIMATE

Ireland's position at the head of the Gulf Stream, which brings warm, moist waters from the Caribbean, means its climate is mild and wet throughout the year. Though the variation is only slight, the west is slightly wetter and cloudier than the east and the south of the

▲ A dense network of fields separated by stone walls in County Kerry. This landscape is typical and has earned Ireland the nickname the 'Emerald Isle'.

country, and more prone to occasional winter storms and windier conditions in general. The mild temperatures and regular rainfall combine with fertile soils to give Ireland some of the best grasslands in the world. The pastures of the southwest are especially prized and are the prime lands for Ireland's beef and dairy industries (see page 30).

IRELAND'S LANDSCAPE

Ireland's climate determines two of its most distinctive and best-known landscape features. The first is the abundance of grass and mosses that gives the 'Emerald Isle' its title. The second is the peat bogs that cover around one-sixth of the country and once covered considerably more. Ireland's peat bogs are formed from the

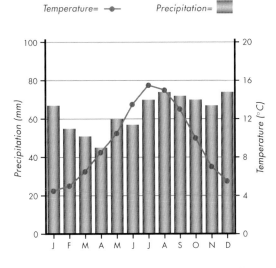

Temperature= ●   Precipitation= ▨

▲ Average monthly climate conditions in Dublin.

remains of decaying plants and animals that sank to the bottom of shallow lakes covering much of central Ireland around 10,000 years ago. Over time this decaying material filled the lakes to a depth of up to 12 metres (40 feet) to create the peat bogs of today. Peat is the earliest stage of the formation of fossil fuels, and can itself be dried and used as a source of fuel. Peat has been harvested at a local scale for hundreds of years in Ireland, but today it is also used commercially. In 2004-5, Ireland opened two new peat-burning power stations at Lough Ree in County Longford and West Offaly in County Offaly. Around half of Ireland's original peat bogs have been cleared for farming, fuel, forestry or other uses, and only about 20 per cent remain in good condition. The pressures on Ireland's peat bogs are today one of the country's greatest environmental challenges (see page 54).

? Did you know?

Many artefacts have been preserved in peat bogs, including jewellery, coins and even an old canoe. These items give insights into Ireland's history. In addition, over 80 human bodies have been discovered preserved in Ireland's bogs, including one dated at over 2,000 years old, found at Gallagh bog in County Galway in 1821.

Focus on: Crossing peat bogs

Water is an essential element of a bog, and on average it makes up 90 per cent of a peat bog by volume. This means that peat bogs are very spongy and present a considerable obstacle to infrastructure such as roads and rail. However, crossing a peat bog is not a new challenge. Archaeologists have discovered the remains of ancient paths across Ireland's peat bogs that date back to 148 BC. These paths, called *toghers*, were made of wooden planks resting across wooden rails – resembling a modern railway track in their design. Corlea *togher* in County Longford is one of the best examples of a *togher* in Ireland.

▶ Cutting peat from bogs near the Wicklow Mountains in County Wicklow, south of Dublin. Peat is harvested for its energy content.

CHAPTER 4

Population and Settlements

Ireland's population in 2005 was around 4.1 million people, up from just under 3 million in 1950. Northern Ireland (part of the United Kingdom) adds a further 1.7 million, but even with this taken into account, the total Irish population is considerably less than it has been historically. This is due to Ireland's long history of emigration, and in particular to the events of the 'Great Famine' of 1845-7 (see box on page 19). Today, however, Ireland's population is growing rapidly as returning Irish and new immigrants arrive to take advantage of the country's recent economic prosperity.

FLUCTUATING NUMBERS

The population of Ireland (including Northern Ireland at the time) grew rapidly during the late 18th and early 19th centuries, increasing from around 4 million in 1780 to just over 8 million by 1840. In 1845 Ireland was devastated by famine and suffered a period of rapid

? *Did you know?*

Ireland has a very youthful population with 25 per cent under the age of 18. This compares with an average of 21 per cent for industrialized countries of the world.

Population data

- Population: 4.1 million
- Population 0-14 yrs: 21%
- Population 15-64 yrs: 68%
- Population 65+ yrs: 11%
- Population growth rate: 1.5%
- Population density: 58.3 per sq km/ 151.1 per sq mile
- Urban population: 60%
- Major cities: Dublin 1,033,000

Source: United Nations and World Bank

◀ Dublin is the most populated city in Ireland and the destination of many returning Irish and new immigrants. This is Grafton Street, one of the city's main retail streets.

population decline, losing a quarter of its population in just a few years. Ireland struggled to recover from the famine and people began to emigrate in large numbers, most of them going to the United States, the UK and Australia. It is only since 1960 that Ireland (separate from Northern Ireland since 1921), then with a population of 2.8 million, has seen any increase in its population. Population growth has been especially fast since 1990, increasing by 17 per cent up to 2005. This is comparable with population growth in the United States over the same period (17.5 per cent), but much faster than in the UK, where growth was just over 3 per cent.

? Did you know?

Since records began in 1820, more than 4.8 million Irish people have been officially admitted to the United States as permanent immigrants, half of this number before 1870. By 2005 the United States had 34 million residents claiming Irish ancestry – more than eight times the population of Ireland in the same year.

▲ Like this young boy celebrating St Patrick's Day in San Diego, California, millions of Americans can trace their ancestry back to immigrants from Ireland.

Focus on: The Great Famine

In the 19th century Ireland was almost completely dependent on the potato as its main food crop. Potatoes grew well in Ireland, but were (and still are) subject to fungal diseases known as 'potato blight'. Outbreaks of blight had troubled Ireland for many years causing several periods of famine, but in 1845 a new form of blight caused widespread devastation. The blight turned the potatoes into an inedible mush, and the disease spread rapidly across Ireland. Farmers were expecting a good harvest in 1845, but when they unearthed their potatoes around half of the crop proved inedible. The harvest of 1846 was even worse with almost complete crop failure, and 1847 was also very poor. Three failed harvests proved disastrous as there were insufficient reserves to support the population and Britain offered little help, too late. The 'Great Famine', as it became known, caused over a million deaths due to hunger and disease and resulted in another million people fleeing the country. The dispersal of Irish people throughout the world can be directly linked to this key event in Ireland's history.

NEW DIVERSITY

Although people of Irish origin can be found across the world today, it is still comparatively unusual to find non-Irish people living in Ireland. The vast majority of the population remain of Irish nationality and at the last census in 2002 accounted for 93 per cent of the populace. People of UK nationality made up the next largest group at around 2.7 per cent (103,476 people) with the United States (11,384), Nigeria (8,969), China (5,842), Romania (4,978) and Spain (4,436) being the next largest minority groups by nationality. However, numbers of minority nationalities are difficult to establish accurately. In 2005, for example,

estimates suggest there may have been over 30,000 Chinese and 50,000 Polish people living in Ireland – many times the numbers on the official census records. Despite data inaccuracies, it is clear that Ireland is becoming a more diverse society and that non-Irish immigrants account for a growing proportion of its populace.

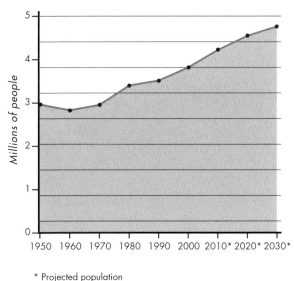

* Projected population

▲ Population growth 1950-2030

URBANIZATION

Ireland is often considered a very rural country, and to some extent this is true. In 2005, 40 per cent of the population remained rural, much higher than in the United States (19 per cent) or the UK (11 per cent). Nevertheless, Ireland is now predominantly urban with 60 per cent of the population living in towns and cities, and

◀ These new arrivals in the southern city of Cork are from Eastern Europe. Thousands of Eastern Europeans have emigrated to Ireland since the expansion of the EU in 2004.

the majority of new population growth occurring in urban areas. Cork, Limerick, Waterford and Galway are all key cities that are experiencing considerable expansion to accommodate urban population growth, but their growth is far outweighed by the capital, Dublin. The Greater Dublin Area includes the counties of Meath, Kildare and Wicklow that surround the city, and it had a population of over 1.5 million in 2005. This number is expected to increase to over 2 million by 2021. This means that Greater Dublin alone accounts for about 40 per cent of the Irish population.

HOUSING

Alongside Ireland's recent population growth there has been a boom in housing. Many cities are expanding outwards on to surrounding farmland, or to merge with other settlements. Inner city areas such as Dublin's former

▲ New housing being built in County Kerry. Ireland is undergoing a housing boom to try and meet the demands of its growing population.

industrial docks are also being redeveloped to provide new housing – much of it luxury city apartments. Despite extensive building programmes there remains a housing shortage and this has driven prices up dramatically in recent years (see page 33). A 2006 poll by the national broadcaster RTÉ (see page 41) found that 90 per cent of people felt house prices were too high in Ireland. Even modest housing is today unaffordable for lower-income earners in the cities, forcing people to move into neighbouring areas and travel into the cities to work. This adds to problems of traffic congestion and is driving up property prices in rural areas too. Public opinion is now growing for the government to intervene in the housing market.

CHAPTER 5

Government and Politics

The continued separation of Ireland from the six counties that make up Northern Ireland means that politics is never far from people's thoughts in Ireland. The political system itself is also frequently under scrutiny, and scandal and corruption never seem to be far from the headlines.

POLITICAL STRUCTURE

Ireland has a two-chamber system of government similar to that of the UK or the United States. The main chamber is the *Dáil Éireann* (parliament) which consists of 166 members elected by popular vote for a five-year term. The smaller Senate or *Seanad Éireann* has 60 members. Eleven members are nominated by the prime minister, six are elected by university graduates and 43 are elected in Senate panel elections. Senate members also serve a five-year term. The Irish head of state is the president who also appoints both the prime minister and the cabinet. Mary McAleese succeeded Mary Robinson in 1997, and won a second seven-year term in 2004. Bertie Ahern also came to power in 1997 as prime minister (*Taoiseach*), and was re-elected to a second five-year term in 2002.

POLITICAL PARTIES

The largest party in Ireland is Fianna Fáil which dominated Irish politics throughout the last century and currently holds 81 of the 166 seats in the *Dáil Éireann*. This is not quite enough to form a government, however, and so Fianna Fáil currently governs in coalition with the eight seats held by the Progressive Democrats. The main opposition parties in Ireland are Fine Gael (31 seats) and Labour (21 seats), and in recent years there has been growth in support for the Green

◀ Leinster House in Kildare Street, Dublin, was built in 1745. Since 1924 it has served as the seat of the Irish parliament (*Dáil*), and as the Senate building when parliament is out of session.

Party (six seats) and Sinn Féin (five seats). Sinn Féin is a controversial party to some because it is associated with Northern Ireland and more specifically with the IRA (see page 13), a terrorist group committed to ending British rule in the north and uniting Ireland. Sinn Féin shares these goals, but its leaders insist it is a respectable political party that does not believe in any form of violence. They point to their vital role in persuading the IRA to give up its armed struggle, finally achieved on 28 July 2005. Today, Sinn Féin is the only party represented across the whole of Ireland (including Northern Ireland) and it is also the fastest growing party in Ireland.

Focus on: The peace process

The Irish prime minister, Bertie Ahern, has been a key figure in the struggle to bring peace to Northern Ireland (see page 13). Together with the British prime minister, Tony Blair, he was instrumental in working with the different political sides in Northern Ireland to reach the landmark Good Friday Agreement (also known as the Belfast Agreement) on 10 April 1998. This set out a path for Northern Ireland to form its own government (the Northern Ireland Assembly) and for greater co-operation with both Ireland and Great Britain. In 2002, disagreements led to the collapse of the Northern Ireland Assembly, but in April 2006 Bertie Ahern and Tony Blair again combined forces to set out a renewed timetable for self-governance and lasting peace.

▶ Bertie Ahern (left), the *Taoiseach* (prime minister) of Ireland, and Tony Blair, the British prime minister, have been key figures in the efforts for political stability in Northern Ireland.

PROPORTIONAL REPRESENTATION

Ireland's politicians are elected using a voting system called proportional representation (PR). Under PR every person over 18 has a single vote to elect representatives in a constituency (a political or electoral district). Between three and five representatives are elected for each constituency. Voters indicate which is their first, second, third choice and so on, voting for as many representatives as they like. When the votes are counted, once a representative has a sufficient number of votes, he or she is elected. The votes are then recounted to take account of voters' second choices. This process continues through third choices and beyond until all the

representatives for a constituency have been decided. This model of PR may seem complicated, but is favoured by Ireland because most voters are thought to get at least one of their preferred representatives elected.

CORRUPTION AND MISTRUST

Political scandals and the alleged corruption of government ministers and politicians have long plagued Irish politics. Many of these scandals have been linked to property deals in which politicians have been paid money by developers, apparently in return for planning favours. One of the best known examples of alleged government corruption involves the former *Taoiseach*, Charles Haughey, who died in June 2006. Two public enquiries have revealed that while in office between 1987 and 1993,

▼ Sinn Féin's Sean Crowe (centre) hugs his wife after being elected for the Dublin South West seat in the Republic of Ireland general elections, May 2002.

Mr Haughey received €11 million (around US$14.4 million) from wealthy businessmen.

IRELAND AND THE EU

Ireland's membership of the EU since 1973 has been a major influence on domestic politics and indeed all aspects of Irish life. At the time of joining, the average Irish person was one of the poorest in Europe with a weekly income of just €38 (US$50), less than two-thirds the EU average. As a result Ireland qualified immediately for massive EU investment. Between 1973 and 2003, Ireland received billions of Euros to invest in economic and social projects ranging from road building and new rail lines to community theatre and unemployment retraining programmes.

By 2003, Ireland had received €34 billion (around US$35.7 billion) more from the EU than it had paid in contributions and the average weekly income in Ireland had reached

▲ A sign for a road improvement scheme, part of the National Development Plan (NDP). The NDP is one of many projects in Ireland to be partly funded by the European Union.

€515 (US$540), among the highest in Europe. In 2004, ten new member states joined the EU, many of them hoping to replicate Ireland's experience. But as there is greater competition for EU funds, Ireland may find itself losing out to newer members. This will place greater pressure on Irish politicians who, until recently, have been able to rely on generous EU funding to deal with challenging domestic issues such as transportation and unemployment.

? Did you know?

On 1 January 2002, Ireland adopted a new European currency, the Euro (€), together with 11 other European countries. The Irish pound (punt) disappeared almost overnight.

CHAPTER 6

Energy and Resources

Ireland has very limited reserves of conventional fuels such as gas and coal to meet its energy needs. As a result 87 per cent of its total energy requirements are met by imported fuels. Non-energy resources are also limited, with farmland and fisheries being by far the most significant assets.

ENERGY HUNGRY

Ireland's economic growth since 1990 (see page 30) has led to a massive increase in energy demands. This is partly driven by new manufacturers and businesses establishing themselves in Ireland, but is also due to rising living standards and increased consumption by the population. Between 1990 and 2004 energy demand in Ireland increased by 59 per cent (for the period 1990-2002 the comparative increase in the United States was 19 per cent, and in the UK 7 per cent). The forecasts for future energy

▼ This unit is used for extracting methane gas from a landfill site in County Clare. The use of gas generated by waste is one of the forms of energy efficiency being promoted by the Irish government.

demand expect growth for the period 2005-20 to slow to around 38 per cent, but this still represents a considerable increase.

ENERGY SOURCES

Historically, Ireland has relied on coal and peat to meet its energy needs. In 1990 coal accounted for 23 per cent of the total energy requirement, while peat provided 14.4 per cent. Since then, these figures have dropped considerably to 12.9 per cent for coal and 3.8 per cent for peat in 2004. The decline in their share of Ireland's total energy requirement is due to the closure of older coal- and peat-fired power stations and to the strong growth of oil and natural gas as alternatives. Over the period 1990-2004 consumption of oil increased by 95 per cent and its share of total energy use increased from 44.5 to 55.8 per cent. Consumption of natural gas grew even faster by 153 per cent, primarily due to its use for electricity generation. The share of total energy use for natural gas rose from 15.4 per cent in 1990 to almost a quarter (24.3 per cent) by 2004.

Future energy forecasts up to 2020 predict that Ireland's use of coal and peat will continue to decline, while oil and particularly natural gas consumption will continue to rise. Ireland has proven reserves of around 19.8 billion cubic metres (69.9 billion cubic feet) of natural gas, and there are several offshore gas fields currently being prepared for commercial extraction. However, the fastest growing energy sector over the period 2005-20 is expected to be renewable energies (see box on page 28) such as wind, wave and hydroelectric power (HEP). If these increase as expected by 146 per cent by 2020, then their share of total energy use will increase to 3.3 per cent, compared to 2.2 per cent in 2004.

▲ A motorist inserts payment into a solar-powered parking meter in Clonmel. The Irish government is seeking ways to increase its share of energy from renewable sources such as solar power.

? Did you know?

As an economy Ireland is relatively good at using energy efficiently. The level of income generated per unit of energy in Ireland is around 1.4 times greater than in the UK, and 2.5 times greater than in the United States.

ELECTRICITY PRODUCTION

Natural gas, coal and oil account for almost all electricity generation in Ireland, but Ireland also imports electricity and this practice is expected to increase in the future. Renewable energies account for an ever-growing proportion of electricity generation and by 2020 are expected to account for 8.3 per cent of electricity, with most of this increase coming from wind power.

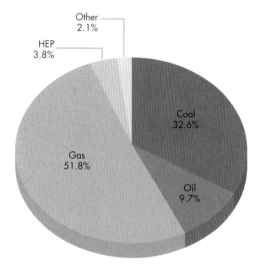

Other 2.1%
HEP 3.8%
Coal 32.6%
Gas 51.8%
Oil 9.7%

▲ Electricity production by type

Focus on: Renewable energy

Ireland's earliest forms of renewable energy came in the form of hydroelectric power (HEP). The first HEP installation at Ardnacrusha, County Clare, was opened in October 1929. There are now several HEP installations in Ireland producing 3.8 per cent of electricity in 2002. However, in 2004, another renewable energy, wind power, produced greater electricity output than HEP for the first time. Wind energy in Ireland has grown from virtually nothing in 1992 to a capacity of almost 500 MW by the end of 2005 (HEP by contrast was 241 MW). Much of the increased capacity in 2004 came from the opening of Ireland's largest windfarm at Meentycat in County Donegal, and its first offshore windfarm located 10 km (6 miles) off the coast at Arklow in County Wicklow. Strong growth continued in 2005 and Ireland has one of the highest wind potentials in the world.

▼ A stone quarry north of Limerick provides stone for use in the construction and road-building industries.

MINERAL RESOURCES

Ireland has commercially viable deposits of several minerals, the most significant of which are zinc, lead and gypsum. In 2005 Ireland produced around 41 per cent of European zinc concentrate and 27 per cent of its lead concentrate. Gypsum mining also received a boost in 2005 with a new underground mine opening in County Monaghan. Copper, gold, silver, barites, dolomite and talc are other minerals that are (or have been) mined in Ireland, although in small quantities.

LAND AND SEA

Ireland's farmland and fisheries have long been an important resource and remain so today. Irish farm products are respected worldwide and fisheries are also important, though less so than in the past as a result of EU quotas on fish catches to conserve stocks. In 2005 the Irish fishing fleet was limited by the rules of the EU Common Fisheries Policy to 55 days at sea per year. The Irish fishing industry continues to modernize, however, with developments such as the recent work on Killybegs port in County Donegal to become the largest seafood port in Europe. Aquaculture (the farming of fish and shellfish) has experienced strong growth since its introduction in the 1970s with output increasing from 26,500 tonnes in 1990 to a peak of 61,000 tonnes in 2002.

▲ A commercial fish farm off the coast of County Kerry. Fish farming accounts for an increasing proportion of Ireland's total fishery production.

? Did you know?

The seven offshore turbines installed at Arklow Bank Offshore Wind Park in 2004 were the largest in the world at the time. Each turbine stands 124 m (406 ft) high and has a rotor diameter of 104 m (341 ft) feet (a jumbo jet by comparison has a wingspan of 64 m/ 210 ft). The turbines produce enough electricity for 16,000 average Irish homes.

CHAPTER 7

Economy and Income

Ireland's economy has undergone nothing short of a revolution since the 1980s, transforming itself from one of the weakest to one of the strongest in Europe. Between 1990 and 2004 for example, Ireland's economy (measured by GDP) almost quadrupled in value, with average annual growth of 6.7 per cent and a high of 10.25 per cent between 1997 and 2000. By comparison, average annual economic growth 1990-2004 for the UK was 2.3 per cent, and for the United States 3.1 per cent.

TRADITIONAL ECONOMY

As recently as 1980, agriculture and industry accounted for 51 per cent of employment in Ireland and 48 per cent of the domestic economy. Agriculture is Ireland's traditional industry and the country is well-known for its high-quality beef and dairy produce. Industry was focused primarily on the extraction and processing of natural resources such as peat and timber, and minerals including zinc, lead, gypsum and copper. Manufacturing industries in Ireland were traditionally small-scale and included textiles, food and beverages.

ECONOMIC TRANSFORMATION

In 1965 Ireland signed the Anglo-Irish Free Trade Agreement with the UK, and in 1973 it became a member state of the EU. These two key events removed trade barriers (such as taxes and quotas on trade) and helped transform the Irish economy, creating new export opportunities for Irish goods. A government body called the Industrial Development Authority (IDA) worked to encourage the growth of industry in Ireland and to persuade foreign companies to locate their operations in Ireland. Engineering, electronics and pharmaceutical industries were among those attracted to set up in Ireland leading to substantial growth in manufacturing and industry at a time when most other European nations were suffering a decline. As a result, manufacturing and industry's share of the economy grew from 35 per cent in 1973 to 41 per cent in 2003. This may seem unremarkable, but in the UK the economic contribution of manufacturing and industry declined over the same period from 42 to 26 per cent, and in the United States from 34 to 22 per cent.

◄ Dorrus Farmhouse cheese is coated in salt water before being packaged and stored. This small cheese factory in Dorrus, County Cork, is one of many specialist dairy producers in Ireland.

Agriculture has been unable to sustain its contribution to the Irish economy, falling from 18 per cent of GDP in 1973 to just 3 per cent by 2003. It remains an important sector, however, employing around 6 per cent of the workforce in 2003 and increasingly specializing in high-value, quality produce, including a growing demand for organic goods.

FOREIGN INVESTMENT

Ireland's geographical location (between the major markets of Europe and North America), educated workforce, and relatively low taxes have attracted many overseas companies to invest in the country since the early 1990s. High-tech sectors such as the computer, software and biomedical industries have been particular growth sectors. For example, in Leixlip, to the west of Dublin, the US computer giant Intel has invested in huge facilities (the biggest outside the United States)

to manufacture microchips. Other well-known high-tech companies with substantial operations in Ireland include Microsoft, Apple and Dell.

▲ These lab technicians wear protective gear to protect the sensitive semiconductors being manufactured at this Intel computer factory in Leixlip.

? Did you know?

Ireland's recent economic success has been compared to that of several Southeast Asian economies including South Korea, Taiwan and Singapore. These economies were called the 'East Asian Tiger economies' and Ireland has since become known as the 'Celtic Tiger'.

Economic data

- Gross National Income (GNI) in US$: 137,761,000,000
- World rank by GNI: 35
- GNI per capita in US$: 34,280
- World rank by GNI per capita: 12
- Economic growth: 5%

Source: World Bank

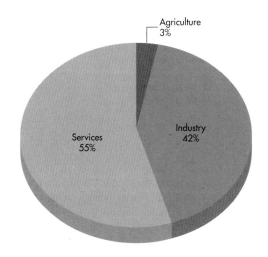

Agriculture 3%

Services 55%

Industry 42%

▲ Contribution by sector to national income

Service industries have also invested heavily in Ireland including telemarketing and tele-services, insurance and banking. In Dublin the Irish Financial Services Centre (IFSC) has been particularly successful (see box).

Though sectors such as IT and financial services are hugely beneficial to the economy, some analysts believe that Ireland is too dependent on foreign investment in these areas, especially as companies could quickly relocate if more competitive locations (such as India and China) emerged. Ireland continues to adapt to these pressures by improving the efficiency and quality of the services and infrastructure needed by such companies.

? Did you know?

More than half of the world's top 50 banking corporations and half of its top 20 insurance companies have offices in Dublin's IFSC. This makes the IFSC one of the world's premier financial centres.

Focus on: The IFSC

The Irish Financial Services Centre (IFSC) was established in 1987 by the Irish government with the approval of the EU. Its aim was to boost the Irish economy by creating a zone in the former docks area of Dublin in which to attract new service industries such as banks, insurance and trading companies. The area's infrastructure was redeveloped and companies choosing to invest in the IFSC were offered a lower rate of corporate tax (10 per cent as opposed to the normal 12.5 per cent) up until 2006. The IFSC has been a great success, and some analysts estimate that over a trillion Euros are now traded through the IFSC annually. Although taxes for IFSC companies have reverted to 12.5 per cent this is still lower than in other European nations such as Germany (38.9 per cent), France (34.33 per cent) and the UK (30 per cent). This means the IFSC remains attractive to overseas investors looking for a European base and is continuing to expand.

▶ Modern office buildings in the IFSC in Dublin. The IFSC has been one of the most successful aspects of Ireland's economic recovery and service sector growth since the mid-1980s.

RISING INCOMES, RISING COSTS

The Irish population has enjoyed a near trebling of its average annual income between 1990 and 2004. By 2004 the average income of around €27,800 (US$34,280) was almost a quarter higher than the average for the Eurozone countries (the 12 countries, including Ireland that share the Euro currency). In 1990 it had been 32 per cent below average. With rising incomes have come rising costs, however, particularly in the housing market. The cost of an average house in Ireland increased from €75,000 (US$87,500) in 1996 to €280,000 (US$370,000) in 2005.

EMPLOYMENT

Ireland presently has low unemployment and actually suffers a shortage of labour to maintain its current strong growth. In recent years this labour gap has been filled by immigration of non-Irish nationals. By October 2005 there were almost 160,000 non-nationals in the workforce, up by 45,000 in a year and representing around 8 per cent of the total workforce. Most non-nationals find employment in relatively low-paid jobs in the catering, hospitality, manufacturing, health, education and agricultural sectors. They play a vital role in the economy and forecasts suggest their numbers will continue to rise, especially following the expansion of the EU to 25 members in 2004. The majority of non-nationals entering Ireland in 2004-5 to find work came from new EU member states, more than trebling their numbers in less than a year.

? Did you know?

The high cost of housing has fuelled housing construction in Ireland and over one-third of all houses in the country were built between 1996 and 2005.

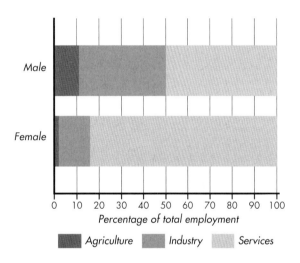

Percentage of total employment

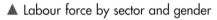

■ Agriculture   ■ Industry   ▢ Services

▲ Labour force by sector and gender

▶ Higher incomes have led to a consumer boom in Ireland. Expensive luxury cars are one of the more visible signs of these newfound riches, but not everyone is sharing in the wealth being generated.

CHAPTER 8

Global Connections

Ireland has always maintained a neutral stance in international relations, playing no part in World War II for example. Ireland does have a considerable international presence, however, particularly within the United Nations (UN) and the European Union. Ireland's role in UN peacekeeping missions is a good example of this commitment to international affairs. Irish troops have frequently played their part including early deployments in 1960s Congo to more recent actions in Lebanon, Sierra Leone and Namibia.

IRELAND'S INTERNATIONAL ROLE

Irish non-governmental organizations (NGOs) also feature heavily in emergency relief, aid and long-term development work around the world. In the early days of the Irish state this was largely confined to missionary organizations involved in charitable and educational work in Africa, Asia and South America. More recently

Irish NGOs and agencies such as Concern, Trócaire, Gorta and Goal have all become major forces in overseas aid and international development. Individuals from Ireland have also played significant international roles including the former president of Ireland, Mary Robinson, who went on to become UN High Commissioner for Human Rights (1997-2002). More populist figures include the musicians Bob Geldof (see box) and Bono from the Irish rock band U2, both of whom have been vocal in campaigns to alleviate poverty in Africa and other developing regions.

IRISH EMIGRATION

The Great Famine (see page 19) sparked mass emigration from Ireland to many parts of the English-speaking world. However, while many people may trace their Irish ancestry back to this event, it was not the first example of Irish emigration. From the late 18th century onwards

◀ Irish soldiers on duty for the UN in Yaroun, southern Lebanon, as part of a peacekeeping force deployed to provide security following the Israeli withdrawal from Lebanon in 2000.

Focus on: Bob Geldof

Bob Geldof began his public life as the lead singer of Irish pop band the Boomtown Rats, but became internationally famous as one of the key organizers of the Live Aid benefit concerts in 1985. Live Aid was motivated by horrific images of suffering during a famine in Ethiopia and resulted in a best-selling record and huge open-air concerts to raise funds for the famine victims. Over US$50 million was given worldwide, saving millions of lives. Since Live Aid, Bob Geldof has remained involved in campaigns to improve the well-being of people living in Africa. In 2004 he became part of a campaign to reduce debt for the world's poorest countries. His involvement included meetings with world leaders such as George W. Bush and Tony Blair. In 2005, 20 years after the original Live Aid concerts, Geldof organized 'Live 8', a series of simultaneous concerts in nine cities worldwide to raise awareness and money to combat global poverty.

▲ Bob Geldof is one of the best-known Irish people in the world thanks to more than 20 years of activity to fight poverty in Africa.

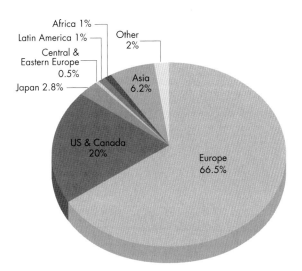

▲ Destination of exports by major trading region

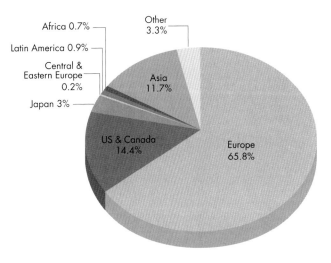

▲ Origin of imports by major trading region

potato-pickers routinely left northern counties such as Donegal, Derry and Antrim to work in Scotland, and emigration to England began in the early 19th century to meet the new labour demands of the Industrial Revolution. Liverpool, Manchester and Birmingham attracted particularly large Irish populations at this time.

Wherever the Irish have emigrated they have created their own communities, blending elements of their own culture with that of their new homeland. This is especially true in North America where a strong Irish-American culture has developed. Many famous and influential people in the United States lay claim to Irish ancestry including presidents (John F. Kennedy, Ronald Reagan and Bill Clinton among them), movie stars and rappers.

▼ Former US president Bill Clinton plays a round of golf at Ballybunion Golf Club, County Kerry, in May 2001. Clinton is one of many famous Americans to trace their ancestry to Ireland.

Beyond North America and the UK, the Irish are found across the world in smaller numbers. One of the first Irishmen to make it to South America was a military man, Colonel Bernard O'Higgins. He is historically important in the continent as his alliance with Simón Bolívar led to the independence of a number of countries including Bolivia, Venezuela, Peru and Chile. The Irish have also been prominent in Commonwealth countries such as Australia and New Zealand. Many of the first Irish to Australia were convicts, sent to the Australian penal colony for petty crime or political beliefs. Indeed the last ship ever to bring convicts to Australia in 1867 was full of rebel Fenians (see page 10).

EXPORTING THE IRISH

Elements of Irish culture such as the welcoming Irish public house (bar) have been exported across the world from the Czech Republic to Cambodia. Another famous export is Guinness, now brewed in different locations worldwide, such as Nigeria and Malaysia. Culturally, Irish music is popular worldwide with numerous big

acts including U2 and The Corrs. The Irish have also demonstrated international sporting achievement in areas such as horse racing, motor racing, golf and soccer. Gaelic sports such as Gaelic football and hurling (see page 50) have their own clubs in Brussels (Belgium), Toronto (Canada) and even Taipei (Taiwan).

NEW CONNECTIONS

Increased prosperity in Ireland together with greatly enhanced global transport and communications are allowing the Irish to form many new connections in the 21st century. For example, Irish investors have become heavily involved in overseas property markets in the UK, Spain, Portugal, Eastern Europe and even South Africa. The return of former migrants to take advantage of Ireland's recent economic growth is also creating new connections and a visible internationalization of Irish culture. This is further enhanced by a recent influx of new immigrants in the 1990s, many of them asylum seekers from various areas of conflict including Bosnians, Somalis and Kurds. More recently newly arrived communities have included large numbers of people from Poland, Lithuania, Russia and China.

On the streets of Dublin, Cork and even the smaller cities, there are now international restaurants and stores that offer a taste of the wider world. It is not unusual to see a traditional Irish pub next to a Japanese *sushi* restaurant and a Russian food store. But the speed with which new communities have emerged in Ireland has also raised some

tensions with local people and integrating the newly arrived into a new multi-cultural Ireland represents a considerable challenge.

▼ The World Irish Dancing Championships are an example of how Irish culture has become global – over half the competitors come from outside Ireland.

Did you know?

John Ford, father of Henry Ford who founded the Ford Corporation of America, emigrated to America after being evicted from Ballinascarty, County Cork, in 1847.

CHAPTER 9

Transport and Communications

Residents and visitors frequently complain about the Irish transport system which is considered outdated and overused. Dublin is renowned for some of the worst traffic in western Europe. Since 2000, Ireland has embarked on numerous initiatives to modernize its transport and communications infrastructure to meet the needs of its growing economy.

CANAL AND RAIL

The Newry Canal (opened in 1742) joined the coalfields near Lough Neagh to the Irish Sea and was the first canal in the British Isles. The last commercial use of Ireland's canals was in the 1950s, as the railways took over. Ireland's first railway, connecting Dublin to the seaport at Kingstown (now Dún Laoghaire), was built in 1838. The rail network reached its peak around 1920 but has declined ever since due to competition from roads. The 1950s and 1960s saw major closures and today's public network of 3,312 km (2,058 miles) provides only key services connecting Dublin and other cities such as Cork, Waterford, Limerick and Sligo. A line between Dublin and Belfast in Northern Ireland, is jointly operated by Irish Rail (*Iarnród Éireann*) and Northern Ireland Railways.

Transport & communications data

- Total roads: 95,736 km /59,489 miles
- Total paved roads: 95,736 km /59,489 miles
- Total unpaved roads: 0 km /0 miles
- Total railways: 3,312 km /2,058 miles
- Airports: 36
- Cars per 1,000 people: 382
- Mobile phones per 1,000 people: 880
- Personal computers per 1,000 people: 421
- Internet users per 1,000 people: 317

Source: World Bank and CIA World Factbook

◀ The M1 motorway at the new Boyne Bridge near Drogheda. This is one of many infrastructure projects to improve transportation in Ireland.

Ireland's earliest rail line between Dublin and Kingstown (now Dún Laoghaire) was one of the world's first commercial passenger lines when it opened in 1838. It is still in use today.

ROAD TRANSPORT

Motor vehicles dominate transport in Ireland today and recent economic prosperity has seen vehicle numbers rise rapidly from 270 per 1,000 people in 1990 to almost 450 per 1,000 by 2004. This has brought significant problems owing to Ireland's relatively small size and poor road network. There are few motorways and with much of the population concentrated in urban areas, traffic there can be especially bad.

The National Development Plan (NDP) is a major government initiative that includes improvements to Ireland's road infrastructure. A primary aim of the NDP is to ensure all main cities are connected by multiple-lane roads by 2015. The M1 motorway linking Dublin to Belfast in Northern Ireland is one of the major NDP projects and by 2006 around two-thirds of this had been completed. When finished in 2010 the M1 is expected to reduce travel time between Dublin and Belfast to less than two hours.

SUSTAINABLE TRANSPORT

Several forms of transportation have been introduced in Greater Dublin to try and reduce car use in and around the capital. The first of these was the DART (Dublin Area Rapid Transit) system, an urban rail line opened in the 1970s to link the northern and southern coastal suburbs. More recently, two light rail routes known as the Luas (meaning 'speed') were opened in 2004. The Luas has been heavily used since its opening, carrying an estimated 60,000 passengers daily. In 2005 Ireland launched a plan called Transport 21 for the period 2005-15 in which the Luas plays a key role. This plan includes linking the two existing lines and extending services through several new lines. A new smart payment card (pre-charged with money to reduce the need for cash transactions) introduced to Luas in 2005 is the first step of an eventual integrated payment system for all public transport in Ireland.

▲ A passenger boards one of the new Luas light rail trams that began to serve Dublin in 2004.

The last tram lines in Dublin closed in 1959, but in 2004 modern trams (Luas) began to run in Dublin once again in order to promote more sustainable transportation.

AIR TRAVEL

Ireland's two key international airports are Dublin in the east and Shannon in the west. Dublin Airport is particularly busy; in 2006, plans were approved for a new runway to cope with increasing demand. Shannon's main international traffic is transatlantic with connections to the United States. Cork and Knock are Ireland's other international airports, dealing primarily with short-haul European traffic. Domestic airports include Sligo, Kerry (Farranfore), Waterford and Galway.

Ireland's national carrier, Aer Lingus, has been in business since the 1930s and flies to a number of European and US destinations. More recently, however, Ryanair has become the better known Irish-owned airline for its major role in revolutionizing air travel in Europe.

? Did you know?

In 2005-6 Ryanair carried around 25 million passengers a year. By 2012 this is expected to increase almost threefold to 70 million a year.

Formed in 1985, Ryanair specializes in low-cost flights to smaller airports across Europe, a successful formula that has made it one of the world's largest and most profitable air carriers.

COMMUNICATIONS TECHNOLOGY

Technology and communications have played key roles in Ireland's economic success. Despite this, public use of the Internet (measured by users per 1,000 people) in 2004-5 was less than half that of the United States, the UK, Denmark and Sweden and lower than in France and Germany. Internet use is likely to increase with the ongoing expansion of high-speed broadband technology across the country.

Four main companies dominate Ireland's mobile phone market which in 2006 had around 4 million subscribers. Mobile phones are particularly popular among the younger generations for both calls and text messaging. In 2006, Irish users sent some 3.6 billion text messages annually.

◄ Passengers disembark from a Ryanair jet. Ryanair has become one of the most influential airlines in Europe due to its low-cost, budget fares.

NATIONAL MEDIA

Ireland's national broadcasting corporation, RTÉ (*Radio Telefís Éireann*), provides two TV channels (RTÉ One and Two) whilst independent channels include TV3 and the Irish language channel TG4. Radio has four national channels from RTÉ, including an Irish language service and a number of local independent channels. The printed media is dominated by the *Irish Times* and the *Irish Independent*, and many UK papers now produce an Irish version.

DIGITAL SERVICES

Digital television is rapidly increasing its share of the market in Ireland bringing hundreds of new channel options, with British-based channels being particularly popular. By 2006, some 28 per cent of the 1,350,000 Irish households with a television had switched to digital television services via cable or satellite.

▲ This touch-screen payphone in a Dublin street also provides Internet access and email facilities.

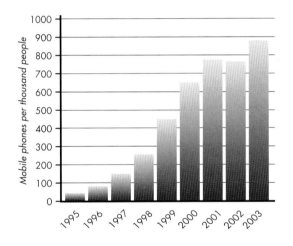

▲ Mobile phone use, 1995-2003

Focus on: Ennis e-town

In the late 1990s the small town of Ennis in County Clare won a national competition to be developed as Ireland's first experimental e-town – an electronic town designed to maximize the use of IT in daily life and interactions. Between 1997 and 2002 a total of €19 million (US$22.2 million) was invested to develop a local town network, completely connected to the Internet by home computer and able to exchange information and services electronically. A total of 20,000 residents, 610 businesses and 13 schools, together with 87 community organizations and two local authorities, took part in the experiment and continue to develop their IT use in the town today.

CHAPTER 10

Education and Health

Ireland's education and health systems are similar to those of the UK and other European countries and provide good standards of service. Both are undergoing changes and modernization to meet the changing demands of the population and the times.

PRIMARY EDUCATION

Primary schooling is provided free by the state across Ireland with most children starting at the age of four or five and attending for around seven years up to the age of 12. An increasing number of children attend pre-schools or playgroups before entering school, but these are privately run and prove expensive for lower-income families. Some primary schools are *Gaelscoil* (Irish language schools) and these have been growing in popularity as there is a renewal of interest in the Irish language. Primary schools were traditionally run by various religious orders, but this is less common today. A new,

government-funded but specifically non-denominational primary system called 'Educate Together' has emerged in recent years. One problem facing all primary schools is the demand for places, especially in Ireland's growing suburban communities that are popular with young families.

SECONDARY EDUCATION

Secondary schooling begins at around 12 or 13 years of age and pupils will typically attend for six years. Secondary school is marked by two main exams. The Junior Certificate is taken after three years of secondary schooling, and this is followed by the Leaving Certificate taken after a further three years. Many students take a 'transition' year after the Junior Certificate to do non-curricular subjects such as archaeology, philosophy, law, and civic and social education, and to obtain some work experience. Most secondary schooling is state-funded but there

◄ Young children pray during a lesson at St Brigid's Girls' School in Dublin. In addition to religious-based schools such as this one, an increasing number of non-denominational schools are opening in Ireland.

► The main library at Trinity College (University of Dublin). Trinity is the oldest and most prestigious university in Ireland.

is a significant fee-paying and private sector and a number of vocational and technical schools that provide a less academic curriculum.

HIGHER EDUCATION

Ireland has seven universities, four of which form the National University of Ireland but maintain independent campuses in Dublin (UCD), Cork (UCC), Galway (NUIG) and Maynooth (NUIM). The oldest and most prestigious university in Ireland is the University of Dublin, better known as Trinity College. This was founded in the 16th century and is located in the heart of the city. The two newest Universities, Dublin City University (DCU) and the University of Limerick (UL) are less than 20 years old. Competition for places at all of Ireland's universities is very high. Ireland also has a world-renowned medical college, the Royal College of Surgeons (RCSI) based in Dublin, which was founded in 1784.

Since the 1970s Ireland has also developed a number of technology institutes around the country that offer degree-level education in a wide range of technical and applied subject areas. Some of the more established technology institutes, such as Dublin Institute of Technology (DIT) and Cork Institute of Technology (CIT), are now major competitors to the universities, attracting an increasing number of students. Carlow, Waterford, Dundalk, Sligo and Athlone are among the other Irish towns with technology institutes.

Education and health

- ▱ Life expectancy at birth male: 75
- ▱ Life expectancy at birth female: 80
- ▱ Infant mortality rate per 1,000: 6
- ▱ Under five mortality rate per 1,000: 6
- ▱ Physicians per 1,000 people: 2
- ▱ Health expenditure as % of GDP: 7%
- ▱ Education expenditure as % of GDP: 4%
- ▱ Primary net enrolment: 94%
- ▱ Pupil-teacher ratio, primary: 19
- ▱ Adult literacy as % age 15+: 99%

Source: United Nations Agencies and World Bank

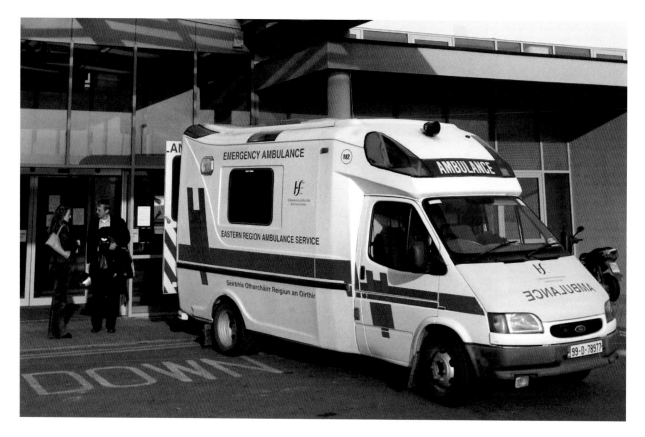

▲ An ambulance delivers patients to a hospital in Blanchardstown, near Dublin.

HEALTH CARE

The standard of health care in Ireland is on a par with other parts of western Europe, but the health care system is the subject of intense public interest as successive governments try to improve organization and efficiency. The main organizations responsible for health care are the Department for Health and Children and the Health Services Executive (HSE) which was created on 1 January 2005. The state provides a basic health care service to all, but almost half the population pays separately for private health insurance. Private care gives people better hospital facilities, such as private rooms, and normally means faster access to medical treatment than in the state system. There are few completely private hospitals in Ireland, however, so nearly all patients (whether public or private) use services provided in public hospitals. This means that patients with private insurance tend to skip the queue and reduce the services available to non-insured patients – a system considered unfair by many. Ireland has around 40 hospitals throughout the country, but as part of the restructuring of health care in Ireland, the government began discussing plans for reducing this to 12 regional 'super-hospitals' in 2003. To date these plans have not been finalized.

PUBLIC AND PRIMARY HEALTH

At a primary care level, most Irish doctors (General Practitioners or GPs) operate as private businesses and are free to locate wherever they wish. The majority of people pay for a visit to the doctor, with the average payment being €40-50 (US$50-63) in 2006.

Vulnerable groups such as the elderly and poor can receive a General Medical Services (GMS) card under a government scheme that provides them with free GP and dental treatment. In addition, the HSE provides free essential medical services to the community such as immunization and health screening (for illnesses such as cancer or heart disease). Social services such as 'meals on wheels' (meals delivered to elderly or home-bound people) or home-help services are largely voluntary, provided and funded by religious and charitable organizations.

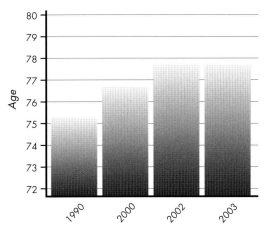

▲ Life expectancy at birth 1990-2003

Focus on: Smoking ban

One of Ireland's most innovative public health initiatives in recent times is the Public Workplace Smoking Ban, introduced in 2004 by the then Minister of Health, Michael Martin. The Smoking Ban (as it came to be known) was intended as a health promotion initiative to improve public health and reduce the inhalation of secondhand smoke by non-smokers. Smoking became banned in all public buildings, bars and restaurants. While many expected the initiative to fail, it has been extremely successful. Most smokers must now leave the premises if they wish to smoke, or go to special outside smoking areas such as those introduced by many bars. The success of Ireland's smoking ban has been closely monitored by other countries in Europe. Scotland introduced a similar smoking ban in 2006 and England will follow in 2007. Other countries are also considering the introduction of a public smoking ban.

◀ Following the ban on smoking in public places in Ireland in 2004, people must sit outside at bars such as this one to smoke.

CHAPTER 11

Culture and Religion

Ireland is an overwhelmingly Catholic country with around 92 per cent of the population professing to be Catholic. However, the number of regularly practising Catholics in Ireland has fallen considerably in recent times. A survey by the national broadcaster RTÉ in 2006 found that only 48 per cent of people attended Mass (the main Catholic service) at least once a week, compared with 81 per cent attendance in 1990.

A highpoint for many Catholics in Ireland was the visit of Pope John Paul II in 1979, who took a Mass that was attended by over a million people in Dublin's Phoenix Park. Many of Ireland's major festivals are associated with Catholicism and St Patrick in particular. One of the main celebrations is the climb of Croagh Patrick in County Mayo, where St Patrick fasted for 40 days in AD 441. The climb takes place on the last Sunday in July and is known locally as Reek Sunday, as this is the local nickname for the mountain.

OTHER RELIGIONS

Protestants make up about 2 to 3 per cent of the population in Ireland, with the proportions being higher in the border counties with Northern Ireland and former planted areas (see page 9) such as Laois and Offaly. Other religions have had only small representation in Ireland, but this is changing as new immigrants bring their religions with them. Islam, Eastern Orthodox Christianity and new forms of African Christianity are all now present, as are various Chinese belief systems. The Jewish

▶ Two nuns help each other as they climb Croagh Patrick, near Westport in County Mayo, during the annual pilgrimage up the mountain.

▲ Irish Jew Raphael Siev runs the Jewish Museum in Dublin and is part of Ireland's dwindling Jewish community. The number of Jews in Ireland has plummeted since the 1950s and is today around 1,100.

population of Ireland has always been small. Once concentrated in an area called 'Little Jerusalem' in the Clanbrassil Street and Portobello districts of Dublin, most Jews have relocated to the suburbs, but the area retains a Jewish museum and old *kosher* bakery.

SECULAR AND SOCIAL CHANGE

The decline in practising Catholics in Ireland, combined with several moral and financial scandals within the Catholic Church since the 1980s, has seen Ireland become a more secular and liberal society. Evidence of this can be seen in the weakening of the once close ties between Catholicism and the governing parties in Ireland. Examples of Ireland's more liberal society include greater use of contraception and higher rates of divorce. Social trends are also reflecting these changes with the proportion of

children born out of wedlock reaching 35 per cent in 2005. Despite these changes, the family is still considered the most important social unit in Ireland and, though less numerous than before, large families are not unusual.

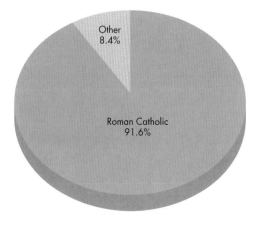

Other
8.4%

Roman Catholic
91.6%

▲ Ireland's major religions

FOOD

Irish cuisine has never been internationally famous and has always tended towards hearty meals based around local ingredients. Potatoes, Irish stew (lamb or mutton, potatoes, carrots and onions), and bacon and cabbage form a major part of the traditional diet. Fish such as mackerel, salmon and Dublin Bay prawns are

▼ The English Market in Cork is well-known for its variety of fresh produce, and increasingly features organically produced food.

important too. A more international range of foods has become evident in Ireland since the 1980s, representing the diversity of cultures now present there. There has also been a renewal of interest in good-quality Irish produce. Dairy products and seafood in particular are exported to select outlets worldwide and sold at local farmers' markets in places such as Dublin's Temple Bar and the English Market in Cork.

FESTIVALS AND TRADITIONS

Ireland's biggest national holiday is St Patrick's Day on 17 March and is celebrated by street parades across the country. The Dublin parade attracts well over a million people. Elsewhere, festivals take place all over Ireland and throughout the year. Specialist festivals have gained a strong following in Ireland. They include the Dublin Theatre Festival in October, the Cat Laughs Comedy Festival in Kilkenny in June and the Festival of World Cultures in Dún Laoghaire in August. There are also some important traditional festivals such as the Puc Fair in Killorglin, where a local wild goat (after whom the festival is named, *puc* being the Irish for goat) is elected as 'King Puc' for the three days of the fair.

THE ARTS

Ireland has a strong arts heritage particularly in literature and drama. Irish writers and dramatists are among the world's best-known and include Bram Stoker, James Joyce, Oscar Wilde, Samuel Beckett, George Bernard Shaw and Sean O'Casey. The Abbey Theatre, Dublin, which opened in 1904, is where many of these writers made their name before going on to worldwide fame. New playwrights such as Martin McDonagh and Marina Carr, whose plays are widely performed in Ireland and overseas, along with novelists such as Colm Tóibín and John Banville, represent the next wave of Irish literature. Ireland has never had a strong film industry, but small budget films made in Ireland have achieved worldwide acclaim including *My Left Foot*, *The Commitments* and *Michael Collins*. Ireland is also popular as a shooting location for film and was the location for the Hollywood blockbusters *Braveheart* and *Saving Private Ryan*.

Focus on: The Irish language

The Irish language, *Gaelige,* is known in Ireland as 'Irish' but is more commonly referred to outside Ireland as 'Gaelic'. It is one of Europe's oldest languages and is closely associated with the other Celtic languages, especially Scots Gaelic and Manx. Once spoken nationally, its use suffered when it was outlawed in public life by the Penal Laws of the late 17th century (see page 9), to be replaced by English. There remain around 100,000 native Irish speakers, concentrated primarily in the western counties of Donegal, Mayo, Galway, Kerry and Cork. This area in which Irish speakers live is known as the *Gaeltacht* and has protected legal status. There are also small *Gaeltacht* areas in Ring in County Waterford and Rathcairn in County Meath. Irish is taught in schools in Ireland and so most people have a good understanding of the language. Despite this, it is not widely used beyond the *Gaeltacht* areas. The language remains strong for cultural, political and identity reasons.

▼ A bilingual (English and Gaelic) road sign in Kinsale, County Cork.

CHAPTER 12

Leisure and Tourism

Leisure and tourism in Ireland are based on its beautiful countryside and its cultural traditions. Ireland's landscapes have broad appeal to visitors and locals alike, whilst traditional sports remain strong and Irish folk music and dance have gained worldwide popularity.

GAELIC SPORTS

The Irish have long been a nation of keen sports followers. The Gaelic Athletic Association (GAA) is one of the biggest organizations in the country with the main GAA sports being Gaelic football and hurling. Gaelic football is played across Ireland with teams organized at club and county level. Women's Gaelic football has become one of Ireland's fastest growing sports in recent years and is currently played by an estimated 100,000 women and girls. Hurling is one of the fastest field-sports in the world and is more widely played in southern Ireland. Although unique, hurling mixes elements of field hockey and lacrosse. It is played with a curved ash stick called a *camán* and a hard ball known as a *sliothar*. Women play a game similar to hurling called *camogie*. The other two GAA sports are handball and rounders. Handball is a game similar to squash, but uses the hand to hit the ball rather than a racquet, while rounders is a game similar to baseball.

Did you know?

Gaelic football was taken with the Irish when they emigrated abroad and today there are Gaelic football teams in London and New York.

◀ Hurling is one of the more popular, and still widely played, Gaelic sports to be found in Ireland and beyond. It is a fast-moving game involving a hurling stick (*camán*) and a ball (*sliothar*).

Focus on: Horse racing

Ireland is perhaps best-known internationally for horse racing in which it has achieved considerable success with both breeding and racing. Racing is now a multi-million-Euro industry. The most famous racecourses in Ireland include the Curragh (for flat-racing) and Fairyhouse and Punchestown (for jump-racing). For many Irish racing enthusiasts the highpoint of the year is the National Hunt Festival held annually in Cheltenham, England, in March. Most of the top jockeys in the UK are Irish and they also ride internationally in places such as Hong Kong, Dubai, and the famous Breeder's Cup event in the United States. The horse-breeding industry is strong and the annual horse sales in County Kildare attract the wealthiest British, Arab, European and American buyers, drawn by the worldwide success of Irish-bred horses.

◀ A horse is paraded during an equestrian show in southeast Ireland. The Irish are renowned for their horse-breeding experience.

OTHER SPORTS

Football (soccer) is hugely popular in Ireland and the national team has qualified for three recent World Cup tournaments in 1990, 1994 and 2002. The team's best performance was reaching the quarter-finals in 1990 under an English manager, Jack Charlton. The Irish team has a huge numbers of followers, with thousands of Irish football fans travelling to support their team when they play overseas. Many of the best Irish players play their domestic football in the English leagues. Rugby Union is another popular sport in Ireland and the national team have won the Five Nations championships (with Wales, Scotland, England and France) on a number of occasions. In most team sports, Ireland and Northern Ireland have separate teams, but rugby is one of a few sports (including cricket, hockey and show jumping) that have All-Ireland teams, with players from both sides of the border.

Water-based activities, from windsurfing to sailing in large ocean-going yachts, are popular participation sports. The wild waves on Ireland's western shores also make it an increasingly popular surfing venue, despite the relatively cold water. Surfing has a growing following with the best breaks off the beaches of Sligo, Donegal and Clare.

MUSIC

Ireland is famous for a wide range of musical styles and artists and these remain popular today. Authentic traditional music is particularly present in the counties of Galway, Donegal, Kerry and Clare in the west of Ireland. In County Clare, Doolin and Miltown Malbay are two of Ireland's best-known music centres. In Doolin, visitors go to local pubs to hear Irish tunes played on fiddles, accordions, guitars and native instruments including *uilleann* pipes and the *bodhrán* – a small skin drum. Some of the biggest names in traditional Irish music are The Chieftains, Planxty, De Dannan, Altan, Sharon Shannon and Danú. Traditional Irish music and dance has gained worldwide popularity, as witnessed by hit shows such as *Riverdance* in the 1990s.

More contemporary Irish music includes leading pop and rock acts, some of which have achieved global appeal. The rock band U2 are by far the best-known Irish act and one of the biggest bands in the world. Formed in the late 1970s by four young Dubliners, U2 performed in Dublin in 2005 for the first time in 16 years to a total audience of 250,000 people over three days. Van Morrison, The Cranberries, The Corrs, Sinéad O'Connor, Clannad, Thin Lizzy and Boyzone are among other international acts

▼ People relax and enjoy playing and listening to traditional Irish music in a bar in Duncannon.

to have emerged from Ireland. This musical legacy feeds a host of musical talent and Ireland's domestic music scene is a thriving industry with attending live concerts a popular leisure activity.

TOURISM IN IRELAND

Tourism has been a significant part of the Irish economy since the 1960s with American, British and European visitors making up the majority of tourists. This is partially a result of historical links, with many British and American tourists returning to visit family members or ancestral homes. Ireland's wild and attractive landscapes and its reputation for friendly and welcoming people make it popular to a much wider audience, especially with the growth in low-cost flights from mainland Europe. Since 2000, however, the Irish Tourist Board has seen the growth in visitor numbers slow down. The reasons include the cost of accommodation, lack of good food, poor transportation and an unpredictable climate. Dublin continues to receive high visitor numbers and has long been the most frequently visited area. One aim for the Irish Tourist Board is to persuade tourists to explore the rest of the country in order to spread both the pressures and benefits of tourism more evenly.

Tourism in Ireland

- 🗁 Tourist arrivals, millions: 6.774
- 🗁 Earnings from tourism in US$: 5,265,000,000
- 🗁 Tourism as % foreign earnings: 4.1%
- 🗁 Tourist departures, millions: 4.634
- 🗁 Expenditure on tourism in US$: 4,832,000,000

Source: World Bank

▲ A tourist finds out about the attractions in the town of Wexford. Improved visitor information such as this is helping to spread tourism beyond Dublin.

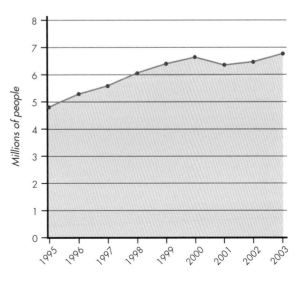

▲ Changes in international tourism, 1995-2003

CHAPTER 13

Environment and Conservation

Despite its modest size, Ireland has a wide range of habitats including forests, bogs, mountains, cliffs, rivers and coasts. Birdlife is prolific as Ireland is an important stop-off point for migratory species, but wildlife is limited with only a few native species. Pressures on the environment come almost entirely from human activities and there are few places in which human intervention is not evident, but Ireland is encouraging the protection of its environment through a range of practical actions.

AN ISLAND TRANSFORMED

Historically, forests and peat bogs would have covered much of the Irish landscape. Beginning in the Middle Ages, pressure for timber, fuel and agricultural land meant that vast areas of forest were felled, peat land harvested and bogs drained. Today original forests cover less than 1 per cent of Ireland's land area, whilst agricultural land (sometimes mixed with forest or other natural habitats) accounts for up to 91 per cent. With natural habitats squeezed into a few remaining pockets, their importance to wildlife and their need for protection becomes increasingly significant. Ireland's protected areas are designated as either Natural Heritage Areas (NHA), Special Areas of Conservation (SAC) or Special Protection Areas (SPA). Much of Ireland's six national parks (Killarney, Glenveagh, Connemara, Wicklow Mountains, The Burren and Ballycroy) includes land designated as an SAC.

One of the problems in protecting land in Ireland is that most of it is privately owned and the government cannot afford to purchase land to set aside for national parks or other forms of protection. To overcome this, government departments work closely with landowners

◄ Stunning scenery at Upper Lake in Killarney National Park. This is one of the three lakes of Killarney, the other two being Muckross Lake (Middle Lake) and Lough Leane (Lower Lake).

▶ Connemara ponies in the countryside at the Bog of Letterdife, near Roundstone in County Galway.

through incentives and management plans. For example, the government is presently working with landowners to plant around 20,000 hectares (50,000 acres) of trees annually between 2000 and 2030, with the hope of increasing forest cover in Ireland by around 1 per cent of the total land area every three years.

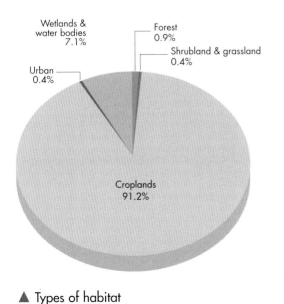

Wetlands & water bodies
7.1%

Forest
0.9%

Shrubland & grassland
0.4%

Urban
0.4%

Croplands
91.2%

▲ Types of habitat

WILDLIFE

Ireland's native birdlife is not diverse by comparison with other European nations, but its coastal waters and wetlands are important habitats for species making their annual migrations between northern and southern latitudes. Ireland has some of the largest colonies of breeding seabirds anywhere in the world including fulmars, petrels, puffins and razorbills, as well as a variety of gulls. The majority of these birds nest on the cliffs of western Ireland, whilst on the east coast wading birds are more common, particularly around Dublin Bay.

Ireland's 25 mammal species include three species of deer (red, fallow and sika), hares, rabbits and the red fox. The Connemara pony is a native Irish horse that has been domesticated into a riding pony. Twenty-three species of whale or dolphin have been identified in Irish waters, with the western coast renowned for good sightings of whales and dolphins, often from the land.

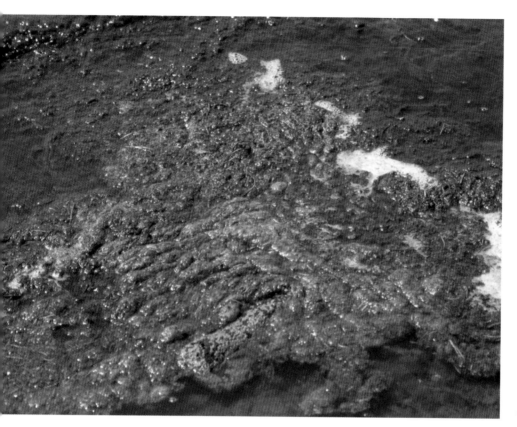

◀ Nitrogenous algae clog the waters of Lough Leane in County Kerry. The growth of algae has been caused by run-off from nitrate fertilizers used on farmland around the lake.

AIR AND WATER QUALITY

Besides habitat loss, the primary threats to Ireland's wildlife come from poor air and water quality. Agriculture, industry and transportation are the main sources of pollutants, and the rapid economic growth of Ireland since the 1980s has seen increased levels of pollution, particularly from transport. Controls on high-polluting fuels such as coal were introduced in the 1990s as a response, and as a result emissions from factories, homes and power stations have declined considerably. Emissions from transport continue to rise, however, and are especially problematic where congestion is a factor. Emissions from congested traffic can be up to 250 per cent higher than when it is free-flowing. Water quality has also shown some improvement in recent years with figures for the last national survey (1998-2000) showing that 70 per cent of rivers and 85 per

Environmental and conservation data

- Forested area as % total land area: 0.9%
- Protected area as % total land area: 1.3%
- Number of protected areas: 104

SPECIES DIVERSITY

Category	Known species	Threatened species
Mammals	25	5
Breeding birds	143	1
Reptiles	6	n/a
Amphibians	4	n/a
Fish	365	n/a
Plants	950	1

Source: World Resources Institute

cent of lakes were in a satisfactory condition. The continued threat to water quality comes primarily from agricultural run-off of pesticides, fertilizers and animal wastes.

WASTE AND RECYCLING

Waste is one of the biggest environmental challenges facing Ireland as it has limited options for disposal. Landfills are rapidly filling up with just 8 years of capacity left in 2005, and incineration has proven unpopular with local communities concerned about toxic emissions. Recycling is central to the government's waste strategy and targets to recycle 35 per cent of municipal waste by 2013 were passed in 2005. There is an extensive network of recycling facilities that includes over 1,900 drop-off centres (for example, in supermarkets), 69 civic waste and recycling facilities and numerous kerbside collection schemes. In 2004 almost half of all commercial waste (much of it packaging materials) was also recovered for recycling or reuse. The government is developing new plans to reduce the amount of waste produced at source, by reconsidering the use of packaging for example (see box). There is also a need to improve the recycling of organic waste which remains poor by European standards.

Focus on: Plastic bags

On 4 March 2002 a new tax on plastic shopping bags passed into law in Ireland. All retailers became obliged to charge shoppers €0.15 (about US$0.20) for each plastic shopping bag they used. The tax was introduced as an incentive to reduce the number of plastic bags entering the waste stream in Ireland, with the money raised from charges being used to pay for a special Environment Fund. The impact of the tax was almost instant, with the use of plastic bags falling by over 90 per cent within three months. Shoppers quickly became used to carrying strong reusable shopping bags that many retailers provided for around €1 (US$1.25) each. The success of Ireland's plastic bag tax is expected to reduce the number of plastic bags used in Ireland by more than one billion every year.

► Most people in Ireland now use strong reusable plastic bags to carry their shopping.

CHAPTER 14

Future Challenges

Ireland has undergone a period of rapid change since the mid-1980s that has seen its economy transformed, its society and culture become more liberal and diverse, and its quality of life improve considerably. It has also seen growing inequalities, increased traffic congestion, rapid population growth and greater environmental pressures. The challenge ahead is for Ireland to balance the rewards of success more evenly and build a sustainable platform for the future.

SPREADING THE LOAD

Dublin has been the engine of economic growth in Ireland for the last half a century and the population is naturally clustered in the Greater Dublin Area, creating enormous pressure on services and degrading both the environment and people's quality of life. In November 2002 the government launched a 20-year plan, the National Spatial Strategy (NSS), aimed at resolving this imbalance. The NSS is designed to integrate the need for greater environmental protection with the continuing need for economic and social development. The key to this strategy is greater regional development to increase the attraction of areas beyond Dublin as a focus for economic activity and living. This will be done through regional incentives to help create employment opportunities, and the strengthening of services at a regional level. If successful, the

◄ An aerial shot of Dublin, showing the River Liffey. A key challenge for Ireland is to spread future growth and prosperity beyond the capital city.

NSS will reduce levels of commuting and therefore congestion, and make the most of Ireland's regional centres, boosting growth sectors such as tourism.

ADAPTABILITY

Vital to Ireland's future will be its ability to adapt to continually changing external influences. The expansion of the EU in 2004, for example, has seen Ireland move from being one of the main recipients of EU aid into an era where it is no longer the most needy member of the EU family. At the same time, the newfound freedoms of the EU are opening Ireland to a new wave of economic migrants coming to Ireland in the hope of finding work in its booming economy. This will place pressure on local services and accommodation and may also lead to increased competition for jobs with local people, especially as newly arrived immigrants may be willing to work for considerably lower wages.

INEQUALITIES

Ensuring that as many people as possible share in the wealth and future of Ireland presents the government with considerable challenges. For example, the health sector is still considered to favour those with higher incomes who are able to afford health insurance. Housing is another area in which inequalities become highly visible, with many lower income families being virtually priced out of the housing market. Policies such as the

NSS and the National Development Plan (see page 39) are designed to reduce inequalities by dispersing the population, and therefore the pressures on housing and services, to areas beyond Dublin, but their impact has yet to be fully realized.

▼ Immigrants from Asia shop in the busy Moore Street Market in Dublin. Refugees and economic migrants continue to add to Ireland's diversifying population.

Timeline

c. 6000-5000 BC Ancient tribes live in Ireland.

c. 3200 BC Newgrange burial monument built.

c. AD 432 St Patrick comes to Ireland and introduces Christianity.

c. 800-1000 Period of Viking invasions and settlement.

1014 Irish High King, Brian Boru, defeats Vikings at Battle of Clontarf.

1169 Anglo-Norman soldiers under King Henry II of England arrive and begin a British presence in Ireland.

c. 1200 English control much of Ireland from their base in Dublin.

1550s Plantations (settlements) in west and south, especially in Queen's and King's counties (Laois and Offaly).

1610s Great Plantation of Ulster.

1649 Drogheda massacre by Oliver Cromwell's forces.

1691 Penal Laws are introduced by the English to suppress and control the Irish (and specifically Catholics).

1742 Newry Canal opened – first canal in British Isles.

1785 The British allow the formation of Grattan's parliament.

1798 Uprising against continued British control of Ireland.

1801 Act of Union makes Ireland part of the United Kingdom.

1821 Ancient bog body (over 2,000 years old) found at Gallagh bog in County Galway.

1829 Catholic emancipation and the end of the Penal Laws.

1838 First railway opens in Ireland.

1845-7 The Great Famine. Potato blight leads to crop failure and the deaths of over a million people.

1867 Uprising against British control by the Fenians who want Irish independence.

1884 The Gaelic Athletic Association (GAA) is founded.

1912 Early plans to allow home rule for Ireland are discussed.

1916 (April) Week-long rebellion against British rule by Irish Republican Brotherhood in which the General Post Office and other prominent Dublin buildings are seized.

1919 Irish political party Sinn Féin declares first independent *Dáil* (parliament) of Ireland.

1919-21 War of Independence between Britain and Ireland.

1921 Ceasefire in the War of Independence leads to the political divide of Ireland into Northern Ireland (remaining part of the UK) and the Irish Free State.

1921-3 Irish Civil War.

1937 Irish Free State renamed Eire.

1949 Eire renamed Republic of Ireland.

1965 Ireland signs Anglo-Irish Free Trade Agreement with the UK to boost its economy.

1968-9 Civil Rights marches by Catholic minorities in Northern Ireland lead to violence with Protestant communities.

1969 British army moves into Northern Ireland to try to restore peace between Catholics and Protestants.

1973 Ireland becomes a member of the European Economic Community (the European Union after 1992).

1979 Visit by Pope John Paul II to Ireland.

1985 Low-cost air passenger carrier Ryanair is founded.

1987 Creation of the IFSC (Irish Financial Services Centre) in Dublin with support from the EEC.

1990 Ireland's football (soccer) team reach the quarter-finals of the World Cup. Mary Robinson becomes the first female president of Ireland.

1993 'Downing Street Declaration' assures Protestants in Northern Ireland of right to vote on any unification with the Republic of Ireland.

1994 Ceasefire announced by the IRA (Irish Republican Army).

1997 Irish President Mary Robinson leaves office to become UN High Commissioner for Human Rights (until 2002).

1998 (10 April) Good Friday Agreement sets Northern Ireland on path to self-government.

2002 Euro currency replaces the Irish punt as the official currency of Ireland. Disputes lead to collapse of Northern Ireland Assembly – UK government retakes control.

2004 European Union (EU) expands from 15 to 25 members. Luas light rail system opens in Dublin.

2005 IRA completes decommissioning of weapons. Cork celebrates being the European Capital of Culture.

2007 European Union (EU) expands from 25 to 27 members.

Glossary

Asylum seeker Someone who seeks shelter from persecution or danger in a country other than his or her own.

Blight A disease of plants (often caused by a fungus) that causes them to wither and die. In Ireland, blight led to the failure of the potato crop in 1845-7.

Catholic Someone belonging to the Roman Catholic Church, which is based in Vatican City and has the pope as the head of the church.

Celtic Relating to a group of languages (and associated cultures) that include Breton, Welsh, Cornish, Scottish, Irish, Gaelic and Manx.

'Celtic Tiger' A term used to describe the rapid economic growth of Ireland since the 1990s and to liken it to similar growth seen in the so-called Southeast Asian Tiger economies of South Korea, Taiwan and Singapore.

Chieftain The leader of a group of people. Used to describe the leaders of Ireland's historical tribal groups.

Civil rights A set of rights that all members of a society should enjoy equally, such as the right to vote, freedom of speech and mobility, and fair treatment from the law.

Coalition A union of two or more political parties which join forces to create a majority that is able to form a government.

Convict Someone who has been convicted (found guilty) of a crime.

Decommission To take something out of working order. In Ireland, often used to refer to the IRA decommissioning (destroying) their weapons.

Depopulation The process by which an area (city, region, country) loses its population.

Discriminate To treat people differently, often unequally.

Emigrate To leave your country of origin to live or work in another country.

Euro A common currency shared by 12 countries in Europe. The Euro was adopted in January 2002.

Fossil fuel One of any energy-rich substances formed from the decayed remains of plants and animals that died millions of years ago. They include oil, coal, gas and peat.

Gaelic Relating to the Gaels (Celts from Scotland, Ireland or the Isle of Man who speak the Gaelic language). Used to describe elements of their shared culture, such as language and sports.

Hydroelectric power (HEP) Electricity generated by the power of water passing through a turbine.

Ice age A period of colder climatic conditions when much of the northern hemisphere was covered in ice.

Incineration To dispose of by fire. It is used as a method of waste disposal.

Infrastructure The transport, communications, energy and other networks and systems that help an economy to function efficiently.

Mass The service of Communion (commemoration of Jesus Christ's last supper) within the Roman Catholic Church.

Migratory Used to refer to birds or animals that regularly travel over large distances as part of their annual survival patterns.

Missionary Someone sent to another country by their church to spread its beliefs or to carry out social work such as teaching or medicine.

Nationalization The process of bringing something (land or an industry for example) under the control of the state rather than private owners.

Nominate To suggest someone for a position of power or control.

Non-denominational Not relating to any religious group.

Non-Governmental Organization (NGO) An organization that operates independently of the government of the country in which it is based.

Paramilitary Describes an organization that is modelled on military principles, but not officially part of the military.

Partition The process of dividing a country into parts.

Peat A fossil fuel composed of decayed plant matter that is high in energy and is burned to generate electricity or heat.

Penal colony A place where criminals were sent to complete their punishment. Australia was originally used as a penal colony by Britain.

Plantation A large estate or settlement controlled by one or a few people.

Presbyterian Relating to, or belonging to, the Presbyterian Church.

Proportional representation (PR) A system of democratic voting in which candidates are elected to office according to the proportion of the vote they receive.

Protestant A member of one of the Christian churches that reject the authority of the pope as the head of the Christian faith.

Republican Someone who believes that Northern Ireland should be politically unified with the Republic of Ireland and cease to be part of the UK.

Ria A physical landscape feature where a former river valley is submerged by the ocean. Rias are common along the west coast of Ireland and account for its craggy indented shape.

Run-off Liquid-based waste (or waste that is transported in water). Run-off is normally generated by agriculture or industry, for example farming chemicals that run into nearby rivers and streams.

Service industry An industry that provides a service to people and other industries. Banking, insurance, transport, education and health care are examples.

Sustainable Something that will still be intact for future generations to enjoy.

Taoiseach An old Irish title meaning 'Chieftain' or 'Leader'. It is the Irish term for the head of government, and is the equivalent of the prime minister in the UK and other countries.

Turbine A mechanical device that is used to convert the movement of water, steam or wind into electrical energy.

Urbanization The process by which a place becomes increasingly dominated by urban (built-up) spaces as opposed to natural landscapes.

Vocational A form of education that provides skills which relate to a particular job or career.

Further Information

BOOKS TO READ

Ireland, the People
Erinn Banting
(Crabtree Publishing Co, 2002)

Ireland, the Culture
Erinn Banting
(Crabtree Publishing Co, 2002)

Ireland, the Land
Erinn Banting
(Crabtree Publishing Co, 2002)

Horrible Histories: Ireland
Terry Deary
(Scholastic Hippo, 2000)

Hunger: The Diary of Phyllis McCormack, Ireland, 1845-1847
Carol Drinkwater
(Scholastic, 2001)

Ireland: A Divided Island
Tony Rea and John Wright
(Oxford University Press, 1998)

Ireland (European Union: Political, Social and Economic Cooperation)
Ida Walker
(Mason Crest Publishers, 2006)

USEFUL WEBSITES

http://www.tourismireland.com
The official government tourist site for Ireland.

http://www.ireland.com
The *Irish Times* online for news and current affairs.

http://www.irlgov.ie
The website of the Government of Ireland.

http://www.cso.ie
The Central Statistics Office of Ireland with up-to-date statistics covering all aspects of life in Ireland.

http://news.bbc.co.uk/1/hi/world/europe/country_profiles/1038581.stm
BBC website country profile of Ireland.

http://www.gaa.ie
The website of the Gaelic Athletic Association (GAA) for information about the different Gaelic sports.

Index

Page numbers in **bold** indicate pictures.

About the Authors

Rob Bowden is a freelance educational writer and photographer with a university background teaching geography and development studies. He has written and advised on many educational books and specialises in global environmental and social issues.

Dr Ronan Foley has been a Lecturer at NUI Maynooth in Ireland since 2003. His specialist areas of interest are historical geography, health geography and Geographical Information Systems (GIS). He has also written books on world health and the River Rhine.